THE BAXTER MODEL

Guidelines for pastoring today

Wallace Benn

Fellowship of Word and Spirit

© Wallace Benn 1993

First published by Fellowship of Word and Spirit 1993

All rights reserved. No part of this publication may be reproduced or stored or transmitted by any means or in any form, electronic or mechanical, including photocopying, recording, or in any information storage or retrieval system, without permission, which should be sought from the publishers, Fellowship of Word and Spirit.

The views expressed in *Orthos* are those of the authors and do not necessarily represent those of the Trustees or Council of Fellowship of Word and Spirit.

Further copies of *Orthos* and information about the Fellowship may be obtained from: Fellowship of Word and Spirit, 7 The Green, Hartford, Northwich, Cheshire CW8 1QA.

Printed in Great Britain by
Tyndale Press (Lowestoft) Ltd., Wollaston Road, Lowestoft, Suffolk NR32 2PD.

ISBN 1 874694 02 8

The Baxter Model
Guidelines for pastoring today

Some books mark you deeply and change your life, although there are not many that you want to read over and over again. Richard Baxter's *The Reformed Pastor*, first published in 1656, is one of those rare life-changing books. In the twenty-one years that I have been in the ministry, I have tried to read this great work on pastoral ministry every five years. I need to, lest I forget what being an under-shepherd of the flock of God is really all about.

Baxter was a salaried preacher at Kidderminster (1641-2) and then vicar of the same town from 1647 to 1661. More than any other, he has been the model parochial minister. His was 'a ministry during which he just about converted the whole town'.[1] His magnificent book is a heartfelt appeal to other Puritan ministers for good pastoral practice, and is an extended discussion based on Acts 20:28, 'Guard yourselves and all the flock of which the Holy Spirit has made you overseers.'

Let me give you a taste of the passion and power of Baxter:

So brethren, watch over your own heart. Keep out sinful passions and worldly inclination. Keep up the life of faith and love. Be much at home with God ... My second exhortation is preach to yourself the sermon that you propose before you preach it to others. When your mind is enjoying heavenly things, others will enjoy them too (p.96).

For he that does not pray for his people will not preach powerfully to his people. If we do not prevail with God to give them faith and repentance, then we are unlikely to prevail with them to believe and to repent ... when our hearts are out of order, theirs will also be out of order (p.18).

We fail to go deeper, to see how we can set these matters forcibly in the hearts of other people. We ought to study how to convince, and how to get inside people, and how to bring the truth to the quick — not to leave it in the air ... few ministers preach with all their might ... What a tragedy it is, then, to hear a minister expand doctrines and yet let them die in his people's hands for the lack of a relevant and living application. Could we speak coldly of God and of men's salvation? So, in the name of God, brethren, labour to waken your own hearts before you come and are fit to awaken the hearts of sinners (p.56).

I know that public preaching of the Gospel is the most excellent means of ministry because we speak to so many at once. Other than that single advantage, it is usually more effective to preach the Bible's message privately to a particular sinner ... I conclude, therefore, that public preaching is not enough. You may study long, but preach to little purpose, unless you also have a pastoral ministry (p.114).

The Baxter Model

> Such personal teaching will make our public preaching so much better understood and regarded (p.106).
>
> When the people see, then, that you love them unfeignedly, they will hear what you say ... and they will follow you the more readily (p.22).[2]

Small wonder then that Jim Packer describes *The Reformed Pastor* as 'another all-time classic, admonishing, motivating, and instructing the clergy'.[3]

The effect of Baxter's ministry at Kidderminster was extraordinary. Packer writes in *Among God's Giants*: 'Kidderminster was a town of some 2,000 adults, and most of them, it seems, were converted under his ministry. He found them, he tells us, "an ignorant, rude and revelling people, for the most part ... they had hardly ever had any lively serious preaching among them." But his ministry was wonderfully blessed.

> When I first entered on my labours I took special notice of everyone that was humbled, reformed or converted; but when I had laboured long, it pleased God that the converts were so many, that I could not afford time for such particular observations ... families and considerable numbers at once ... came in and grew up I scarce knew how.

'Here is Baxter's retrospect of what went on:

> The Congregation was usually full, so that we were fain to build five Galleries after my coming thither.... [The Church would have held about a thousand without the galleries.] Our private meetings were also full. On the Lord's Days there was no disorder to be seen in the Streets, but you might hear an hundred Families singing Psalms and repeating Sermons, as you passed through the Streets. In a word, when I came thither first, there was about one Family in a Street that worshipped God and called on His Name, and when I came away there were some Streets where there was not past one Family in the side of a Street that did not so; and that did not by professing serious Godliness, give us hopes of their sincerity. And those Families that were the worst, being Inns and Alehouses (*sic*) usually *some persons* in each House did seem to be religious.... When I set upon Personal Conference and Catechising them, there were very few families in all the Town that refused to come.... [Baxter asked them to call at his home.] And few Families went from me without some tears, or seemingly serious promises of a Godly Life.

'What Baxter refers to here is the practice which he describes and commends in *The Reformed Pastor*, [...] of systematically interviewing families for the purpose of personal spiritual dealing. Baxter met families in this way at the rate of seven or eight a day, two days a week, so as to get through all 800 families in the parish every year. "I first heard them recite the words of the catechism [the *Westminster Shorter Catechism* was the one he used] and then examined them about the sense, and lastly urged them with all possible engaging reason and vehemency to answerable affection and practice. I spent about an hour with a family." His testimony to the value of this practice is emphatic. "I find we never took the rightest course to demolish the kingdom of darkness till now.... I find more outward signs of success with most ... than of all my public preaching to them."'[4]

Is Baxter relevant today?

As I read this stirring story, I found myself moved and challenged. Certainly the times have changed, and the willingness of people generally to undergo such a 'personal conference' would be very much less in the secular world of our day! Yet I found myself admiring Baxter's practice and constantly asking myself whether there is a way of doing this today. I was convinced of the benefit to pastor and people of such a practice, but wondered whether it was still feasible. Was there a way to adapt and update it?

I became increasingly convinced that people needed pastoring which was as thorough as this, and that there was a lot of confusion amongst the Lord's people about how to work out their faith, given the challenges and pressures of modern living. Although I believed passionately in the priority of preaching (and still do), and how basic pastoring is done through preaching and teaching, I was beginning to see that, like Paul, I must take every opportunity to minister the Word and not just be a pulpiteer.

How could this be achieved? Much pastoral work is done traditionally by visiting families but in many areas this has become difficult. Afternoon visiting is the traditional practice but, increasingly, who is at home? If anyone is, it is usually the mother, and how appropriate is visiting that never reaches the man in the family? Furthermore, I often found that much goodwill was created by my visiting, but it was hard to have any serious spiritual conversations when the TV was left on and you might find yourself battling against 'Neighbours' or the children's need for tea!

The following pages record my attempts, however inadequately, to learn from Baxter's model and to try and adapt his method in two different situations in which I have served. The first occasion was with a large youth fellowship, and the second concerns my present parish ministry.

When I was a curate in Cheadle, Cheshire, I was privileged to be the leader of a marvellous and rapidly growing youth work. At its peak, the youth fellowship numbered over two hundred — their ages ranging from fifteen to twenty. We were desperately short of leaders and so we began choosing and training some of the older young people to help. Each week it seemed that people were being converted, and our evangelistic efforts, by God's grace, were attracting lots of interest and attention. How were these folk to be adequately pastored? How were they progressing? Numbers, especially with young people, can be deceptive. We

The Baxter Model

had a conversational Bible study which I led each week and which had over sixty coming to it. Although it broke all the rules of group dynamics it worked wonderfully! (Indeed I would say that those Wednesday Bible studies were the most exciting, stimulating and encouraging experiences of my life as a minister.) There was teaching and a great deal going on, but what about one-to-one contact?

With a group which was eager to learn, coming from a wide variety of backgrounds and representing no less than twelve secondary schools, surely here was a situation in which I could try Baxter's insights. Thanks to my rector, I had the space to create my own system of pastoral care for what was becoming a large church within a church. So I decided to invite each member of the youth fellowship to come and see me for half an hour. I wondered how they would take it. Would people refuse to come, and would it have a very heavy image? I set out to correct some bad impressions before they could take root, playfully calling it my 'surgery' and assuring them that there would be no amputations! I emphasized that I wanted to get to know each one of them because each one mattered, and that I would not buttonhole them or embarrass them. However, I made it clear that I wanted to talk with them about their relationship with the Lord and to try to help them with any questions and problems they might have.

I found out rapidly that I needed a 'secretary' to make the appointments and chase up people, because that was a job in itself. I asked for a volunteer to help, and one of the star girls in the fellowship volunteered! She did an excellent job, giving me a list of people each weekend for the coming week and arranging all the times on the basis of the days which I had free. Over the next weeks I saw people after school on four days a week from four o'clock until six, and on Saturday mornings from nine until one. The next six or more months were exhausting but very exciting, and although I tried to do too much in the early days, I learnt from my mistakes! It was a great encouragement. As far as I know, nobody refused to come, and the fellowship and assistant leaders prayed faithfully for it.

What were the results? In spite of my inadequacies, there was a noticeable increase in spiritual 'seriousness' amongst members of the group. I found those who were not yet Christians and who needed and wanted help to find Christ. I discovered the hidden problems and heartaches behind smiling faces, and was able to discuss real questions and problems which were holding people back. I found that, once over the initial hurdle of coming to see me, people were more than willing to talk. It began to be known that 'surgery' was 'OK' and that I wasn't too much of an ogre! People became more willing to come and see me and other leaders with their problems, or just to ask for advice. During this time the fellowship grew markedly in spiritual depth and continued to grow numerically, and I became more convinced than ever that Baxter had much still to teach us. So the results of that time with young people were very encouraging (see Appendix II for my colleague's experience with young people today). However, young people are adaptable and teachable — would it work with adults?

My next parish in the Potteries was very different, with a church turning in an evangelical direction in an old village-type mining-town. God graciously blessed the work, and the congregation became a growing and lively village church. Yet in the time that I was there, the 'Baxter method' never seemed quite suitable.

At present I am vicar of St Peter's, Harold Wood, in suburban north-east London, and it is here that I have used, and am still using, 'Baxter's method' with adults. Though my experience may not be appropriate for every parish situation, I hope you will at least ask the question, 'Could I do it here — would it help where I am?' I hope, too, that you will learn from some of my mistakes! I have been learning as I have tried to put Baxter's insights into practice.

The method adapted

I became convinced that Harold Wood was an appropriate place to try this method. The congregation is large (over 500) and it would be a long time before I got to know people really well, but here was an opportunity to get to know them better. Although some 80 per cent of the congregation is indigenous, there are others who come from outside the parish, and it was unlikely that I would ever get around to everyone unless I tried this way. Harold Wood also has a history of being willing to experiment with new ideas when convinced that they are helpful.

After much prayer, I launched the idea at the annual houseparty one September. I told everyone that I wanted to get to know people, that in a large church this was not easy, and that this idea was a way to help. I reminded people that each was important and that, if I could, I wanted to help them spiritually. I said that I believed the Lord had laid this on my heart, and I asked them to pray for it and to seek to minimize any misunderstanding or criticism of it which might arise. Learning from my experience in Cheadle, once again I nicknamed it my 'surgery'.

Furthermore, I told people that I was going to work through the electoral roll of the church and, being Irish, I was going to do it backwards! There was motive in my madness. If you start with 'A', it is a long time before you seem to be making progress, and months later you may still be on 'C'. If you start with 'Z', how many members of your congregation have a surname beginning with that letter? Your passage up the alphabet is rapid, and a lot of progress seems to be made very quickly. This is important in the early days, since there is a great deal of interest and also a considerable amount of speculation about what will be said to particular people!

The Baxter Model

As we saw earlier, it is essential to have a 'secretary' to make all the arrangements. They can often get complicated, with people having to cancel for good reason, and it is important that someone other than the pastor handles this. A fine Christian woman, who helps part time at the church office, has taken this on as her principal area of concern. Each week she gives me a list of those coming . I give her my availability as far ahead as I can, and she works out the rest. On individual cards are brief family and work details if known, plus space for me to make short comments which I keep and file away afterwards. Cards are filled in after people have left — not at the time.

What happens at an interview?

When people arrive they are given a cup of coffee or tea — something to make them feel relaxed and at home. I always ask husbands and wives to come together if at all possible, even if one partner is a known unbeliever. This shows interest in, and concern for, their marriage. If, of course, the other partner does not want to come, that is accepted. If a babysitter cannot be arranged or the children want to come, they are welcome to do so, and my dear and sometimes longsuffering wife looks after them in the other room! This emphasizes that the interview is a joint effort. People like to meet her, too — maybe more than me!

Everyone is asked to come for only half an hour, since I think that anything longer is too threatening. I have learned, having become famous for backlogs or 'surgery queues', to allow three quarters of an hour for each appointment.

Though I have been light-hearted about the way in which a visit is set up, I am clear as to its purpose: to get to know people better, to ask them how they are progressing in the Christian faith, and to give them an opportunity to ask me anything they want. Because of the impossibility of visiting everyone at home, I have asked them to be so kind as to come and see me, and that is very important. If you visit them, you may never get beyond small talk. If it is a visit to me with a stated purpose, it is easier to have a spiritual conversation. This is expected, and is one of the things that I have learned 'by chance'.

People often ask, 'What do you say?', and before I set about the task, I asked myself the same question. What you say needs personalizing, and others may do it far better, but this is what I have found helpful. To begin with, we chat for about five minutes or so. I try to get to know their family and work details, and any problems which they may be facing. Then I have found that really I need only to ask them three questions, since these three questions open up three key areas.

The first question is, *When did you become a Christian?* It is important to note that the question is not 'Are you a Christian?' The first version is gentler, gives the benefit of the doubt, and finds out the same information. When people begin to answer, you soon find out whether they are or not. Dependence upon church or family background — without a personal, saving faith — can usually be spotted quite easily. Once this is established, then that whole area can be addressed. If the person is a believer, it does them good to tell their story and I rejoice with them. If they are unclear or unsure, this can be addressed. Sometimes a 'Discovering Christianity' course, or a visit to discuss matters further with me or with another member of the team, can be suggested. For unsure Christians, suggestions can be made about books to read, or the teaching of 1 John on assurance can be briefly explored.

The second question is *How is your Christian life going — are you encouraged or discouraged, and do you have any problems or questions that are holding you back?*. It is in this whole area that we can discuss walking with God daily by reading the Bible and by prayer. In particular I ask them whether they belong to a home Bible study group or fellowship group and emphasize the importance of supplementing Sunday worship and teaching with an opportunity to learn and to ask questions about the faith in a group setting. It is also true that, in a larger church situation, belonging to a study group is a great way of getting to know some other Christians really well and enjoying rich fellowship together. I urge them to belong to such a group and, if they do belong, I ask how their group is getting on. With most people this is the main area to address, as it encourages them to get the necessary help and support that they need. It is the key area of spirituality and Christian living.

If you look at Ephesians 4, you will see that the way in which Christians grow is by learning (vv.11-12) and by serving (vv.12,16). So the third question is *What are you doing to serve the Lord in the church family and in the world — what are your gifts and/or how can we help you find and use them?'* (We are beginning to run a 'Networking' course to help people find and use their gifts.) I also spend time in encouraging people to see their job and their family as their calling, and the primary area where God calls us to serve him. Through all the conversation I am seeking to encourage a practical acknowledgement of the lordship of Christ over every area of life.

All these are really *areas* of question, and I do not follow a rigid system of certain things to get through: rather, I use these areas as a framework for the matters which I want to raise. We may of course never get past question one! We pray together at the end (I pray, then remain silent for a few moments so that they can pray too if they want to). Finally, I encourage them to talk to their home Bible study leader or to see me again if we can be of any further help. The fact that others are known to be coming, and are heard arriving, makes us disciplined with the time! On leaving I give them a copy of 'A Spiritual Life Check-Up', which a friend brought to my attention (see Appendix 1). It comes from *Leadership*

The Baxter Model

magazine, and I urge people to use it and compare notes, telling them that it is fun but that it does ask all the right questions and is important.[5] I explain that I do not want to see the results (I have known pastors who ask people to do it in advance and bring it with them — I admire their courage but I think that it is needlessly threatening). I do suggest that they talk over the answers with me if they wish — most do not!

These talks with people are relaxed and yet concern eternal issues. So they are very tiring and draining. When I began in Harold Wood, I tried to see twenty couples a week. That was folly, but it helped me get through the long list. Now I try to spend one evening a week doing this, if at all possible. Recently that has proved difficult, with many emergency pastoral needs requiring time, but one night a week, or an occasional Saturday morning, is my normal pattern at present.

Surprises

There have been many lovely surprises. The greatest, perhaps, is that no one to my knowledge has refused to come! And other things have happened. Let me refer to three incidents among many.

On one occasion a husband and wife came to see me, although the husband was not yet a believer. I knew this because we had talked about it together, and I began our session by saying how grateful I was that he had come, as I knew he was not yet a Christian. He said to me: 'Don't bother talking to my wife, she's fine. Talk to me because I need it and I'm worried!' What a God-given opportunity! We had a good conversation and have had several since then.

Secondly, I think of a conversation with a dear brother in Christ who was getting on in years and who was troubled about his area of service in the church. Did I still want him to carry on? He wanted to, but was it still alright? I was able to reassure him and tell him frankly how greatly we valued what he did, and I heard that he went home overjoyed. The next day he died. It was so good to have talked with him on that occasion, and how precious that conversation became! We had shared the joy of being believers together and the privilege of serving God; and his wife, who has had to face the sad loss, was there for the conversation. How good, though sad, it was to be able to quote that conversation at the funeral service.

Thirdly, I had an important conversation with a woman a week before she died, about things that were troubling her, and in God's good mercy she was encouraged and apparently helped. Again, it was good to be able to refer to it carefully at her funeral. The only problem was that at one period it seemed that everyone I saw was doomed to die. My surgery was beginning to appear to have the kiss of death!

Problems

There have been few. Sometimes people come with a list of questions and attempt to set their own agenda, but that does not often happen. My response is to let them continue for fifteen minutes, and then say that they have had a good innings and isn't it about time we changed ends because I have a few questions I would like to ask them. It is surprising what you can get away with if you say it with a smile on your face!

Benefits

1) Once people have been over the threshold of your home, it is easier for them to come again if they have a real problem. I believe that it also encourages people to be more open about their faith, bringing out the challenges they face as well as the joys.

2) It helps us to minister the Word of God in a very personal way and to be able to apply it very directly. It enables us to talk about really important issues and to see who really needs help (not just the ones who are always asking).

3) It sharpens your preaching, as you get to know a congregation better and understand the real problems they face. It helps your consideration of which Bible book to preach on next (pick the one that most relates to your situation) and also is a great help in working out application. Of course no confidence is broken, but we become more generally aware of the areas of challenge or difficulty that people are facing. We see, too, where they are spiritually and what encouragements and warnings they need.

4) Too many preachers do not like people, and can remain aloof from people while defending this attitude by their view of the priority of preaching. I believe that passionately too but, as Baxter said, how will we preach effectively if we do not know the real joys and problems of our brothers and sisters. This is a particular danger for the senior pastor in a large church, who can, by virtue of his job, become distant from his people. Priority time must be made and kept in order to preach well to the congregation, and too many personal demands can dangerously swamp that, but it is bad for a preacher not to know his people.

5) There are others to whom people can be referred, and it is essential to have a small back-up team. This helps the church to function better and enables leaders to see what would most help people in the programmes of the church.

6) Unused gifts and talents can be spotted and encouraged for use in the Lord's service.

The Baxter Model

7) Problem areas in a congregation can be noted. For example, I have noticed how many lonely people we have, even though we have the reputation of being a very friendly church.

8) I believe that it can raise the spiritual tempo in the life of a church.

9) People see that their minister cares. One person said to me, 'You are the first minister to care'. This was very far from the truth, and a compliment that I would not take too seriously. There may be many more who do not think that I care enough, or as much as someone else, but it does make a comment about the perception of how caring we are.

10) It encourages prayer as we see the grace of God in people's lives (thanksgiving), as we see how weak is some people's hold on the things of the Lord (petition), and as we see a mutual growing affection for the Lord, his people, and his ways (adoration). It encourages a minister in humble dependence on God, and I believe also encourages our congregation to pray for us as we seek to pray for them.

Some questions remain

1) Am I seeking to take all pastoral care to myself — what about the pastoral care of home groups? This form of care, it seems to me, is the basic pastoral care unit in a congregation, and nothing I have said above seeks to detract from that. But a Christian needs access in an emergency to his or her pastor, and the 'Baxter method' encourages that. It also provides a supplement to the basic pastoral care of groups, to the benefit of both pastor and people. We take home-group pastoring seriously, delegating pastoral care to the groups and urging them to take it seriously, especially the bearing of one another's burdens. All this is light years away from 'heavy shepherding', and seeks rather that unobtrusive pastoral care which constantly points people to the Good Shepherd and the wisdom of his Word written.

2) Might I not be swamped by all this? Will I keep on doing it? I have not yet been through all the electoral roll membership of the church, so the queston is premature! We have a staff team here which is now committed to this pattern and with whom I can gladly share the task (Baxter shared the task with his curate). However, in going through for the first time, I have felt the need to do so myself. Later it can be shared with the staff and pastoral team.

✳ ✳ ✳

You will realize by now that I am sold on Baxter's ancient wisdom, but read *The Reformed Pastor* and make up your own mind. You may want to adapt his wisdom differently, but I have found that people are very interested in his pattern. Ask yourself the questions, 'Could I do it where I am?' and 'Would it be helpful?'. If it is at all possible, *do it*, because there is still a lot of mileage left in it!

Let Baxter have a last word:

> Such personal teaching will make our public preaching so much better understood and regarded (p.106).

> Ministerial work must be done purely for God and the salvation of his people. It can never be done for any private gain of our own (p.13).

> When the people see, then, that you love them unfeignedly, they will hear what you say...and they will follow you the more readily (p.22).

> It makes me leap for joy to anticipate what pastoral work, when it is well-organized, can produce. Truly, my brothers, you are priviledged in such a work (p.105).[6]

May God the Son, the good Shepherd of the sheep, be glorified by pastoral care that teaches his Word and rejoices in his Gospel, with a deep love for those for whom he died.

The Revd **Wallace Benn** *is vicar of St Peter's Church, Harold Wood, Essex. The substance of this paper was given at a leaders' seminar at Word Alive Week, Pwllheli, 1993.*

NOTES

[1] J.I.Packer, *A Man for all Ministries,* St Antholin's/Bishopsgate Lecture 1991 (St Antholin Trust, London 1991), p.3.

[2] Richard Baxter, *The Reformed Pastor,* abridged edn (Multnomah Press, Portland, Oregon 1983).

[3] Packer, op. cit., p.3.

[4] J.I.Packer, *Among God's Giants* (Kingsway, Eastbourne 1991), pp.53f.

[5] Dennis Wayman, 'A Spiritual Life Check-Up', *Leadership,* vol.4, no. 4 (Christianity Today, Chicago, Illinois, Fall 1983), pp. 88-100. Anyone wishing to reproduce the questionnaire for use, should contact the publisher of *Leadership.*

[6] Baxter, op. cit.

APPENDIX I

A SPIRITUAL LIFE CHECK-UP

Discovering spiritual illness must precede the cure.

As your pastor, I am responsible for your spiritual health in much the same way as your doctor is responsible for your physical health. Both of us must be allowed the privilege of helping you. Often, unless a disease so overcomes us that our doctor or pastor is made painfully aware of it, there is no regular time when I can sit down with you and discuss the health of your spiritual life.

Therefore I am requesting an appointment with you. I am requesting that you do the following 'lab work' not as a test, but as a tool for diagnosis, so that we might know your 'blood count' and decide together on a proper diet and exercise programme that will bring about your best spiritual health.

Since pastors (or doctors) can help only if we allow them, this is entirely voluntary, but I am suggesting that you:

1. Set aside an hour of uninterrupted time in which to thoughtfully answer these questions.
2. Keep your answers only to yourself, to be shared with me and God alone.
3. Make an appointment with me for a one-hour spiritual check-up.
4. Get your 'lab work' answers to me a week in advance for my preparation.
5. Prayerfully and openly meet with me, trusting God to use this experience for you.

A CONFIDENTIAL SPIRITUAL-LIFE CHECK-UP

I. **Blood Type:** Are you now a Christian? .... Comment on your answer: ....
    ....
    ....

    Have you been baptized? .... When? .... Where? ....

II. **Red Blood Cells** (oxygen carriers that prevent anaemia)
    A. Devotional life
        1. How meaningful is Sunday morning worship to you? ....
           ....
           ....

        2. How meaningful is private worship to you? ....
           ....
           ....

        3. Do you feel you are becoming more acquainted with God? .... In what ways? ....
           ....
           ....

        4. Is meditation a part of your spiritual walk? .... Describe ....
           ....

    B. Intellectual life
        1. Are your doubts and questions being answered? .... If yes, how? ....
           ....
           ....

        2. Do you feel you know the Bible? .... What help do you need? ....
           ....

        3. Do you understand basic concepts of theology — justification, regeneration, sanctification, gifts of the Spirit, etc? .... What help do you need? ....
           ....
           ....

        4. In what areas of intellectual life (explaining your faith; theology; practical applications; Bible knowledge; body life; etc.) are you strong, and in which are you weak? ....
           ....
           ....

III. **White Blood Cells** (disease fighters for inner spiritual cleansing and renewing)
    A. Do you feel you are a more accepting, forgiving, loving person than you have been? ....
       Expand: ....
       ....

B. Do you feel you are stronger against temptations (to be impatient, angry, greedy, lustful, etc.)? .... Expand: ....
....

C. Do you feel your self-esteem is healthy? .... Expand: ....
....
....

D. Do you see yourself becoming more pure in motive, thoughts, and lifestyle? ....
Expand: ....
....

E. Do you find yourself usually encouraging others or competing with others? ....
Expand: ....
....

F. Do you occasionally tear another person down in jest or in anger? ....
What triggers this? ....
....

G. How is the Holy Spirit helping you become whole? ....
....
....

IV. Platelets (blood clotters that stanch the wounds of living in a hurting world)

A. Have you found someone to help bear the burdens of life? .... Expand: ....
....

B. Do you find you can share your inner joys, hopes, and dreams? .... Expand: ....
....

C. When someone in jest or in anger tears you down, how do you handle it? ....
....

D. When you fail, what happens within you? ....
....

E. When you succeed, what happens within you? ....
....

V. Blood Pressure (hypertension and exercise)

A. Are you able to turn your finances over to God and tithe, trusting him to supply? ....
   Expand: ....
   ....

B. Are you able to turn your vocation over to God to use you how and where he wants? ....
   Expand: ....
   ....

C. Are you learning to let go of the desire for things? .... Expand: ....
   ....
   ....

D. Are you able to exercise your gifts within the body of Christ? ....
   What do you see as your gift(s)? ....
   ....

E. Are you able to explain to others in the community why you are a Christian? ....
   Any problems here? ....
   ....
   ....

F. How much are you concerned for those who are less fortunate, wanting to share with them the gospel and the helping hand? ....
   ....
   ....
   ....

G. How concerned are you with injustices and other social evils? ....
   ....

VI. Tired Blood (from imbalanced spiritual diet)

A. Is your life balanced? How do you deal with pressure? Do you have regular time for family, recreation, personal growth, etc? ....
   ....
   ....
   ....

B. Do you feel you have a balance of worship, study, and service to stay in shape? ....
   Expand: ....
   ....
   ....
   ....

APPENDIX II

Using the 'Baxter Model' with young people

> When a minister knoweth not his people, or is as strange to them as if he did not know them, it must be a great hindrance to his doing them any good.[1]

So says Baxter of personal ministry, and this, surely, is as true for the youth fellowship as it is for the whole church. It is quite clear that the pastor who knows his people, their problems, temptations and sufferings, knows better how to preach and apply God's Word to them. Yet how are we to put this into practice? With the various demands on the time of the youth leader, who may often also be the assistant pastor, how is it possible, indeed how valuable is it, to embark on personal 'one-to-one' ministry of the kind Baxter recommends? The experience we have had in using the 'Baxter Model' has been very positive.

The first hurdle we had was how to introduce the idea to the group. Our CYFA youth fellowship is a mixed group of boys and girls, Christians and non-Christians, church family and non-church family. We decided to call what we were to do our 'CYFA surgery', with our youth worker seeing the girls and my seeing the boys. Splitting the sexes in this way was generally more helpful. We introduced the idea to the group at one of the main weekly meetings by saying: 'This is an opportunity to say all those things you've wanted to for ages but never had the chance or the courage. We would really like to see how things are going with you, to find out whether you have any problems, and to get to know you a bit better.' We also outlined that this was an ongoing project with the adults in the church. At the end of the evening we signed up a number of people, the best time for meeting appearing to be late afternoon after school or college.

It seemed from the outset that there should be a structure to the 'surgery'. In most cases this was determined by the set of leading questions outlined below. However, the structure was not rigid and often the conversation led away from the plan.

1) When did you become a Christian?

This question, obvious, but deceptively simple, opens up straight away where someone is spiritually: whether professing faith, seeking, or perhaps unconvinced of the truth of the Gospel.

2) How do you feel about Sunday church?

Again, this brings to light the spiritual state — is there a hunger for God's Word?

3) Are you spending daily time alone with God?

4) Are you finding your doubts and questions answered?

This now begins to bring out any specific problems there may be.

5) Do you have any particular problems?

This is deliberately vague — concerns and worries might not just be 'spiritual'.

6) How do you find being a Christian? Do you have any particular temptations?

7) What are your plans for the future?

This draws out how far they see God's involvement in their lives and often leads into talking about gifts and further service.

After meeting with a number of young people making use of this scheme, the benefits have become very clear:

1) It has been enormously helpful for 'spiritual diagnosis'. One to one, away from the peer group, it quickly emerged whether the young person had genuinely understood the Gospel and the claims of Christ on his life.

2) Again, away from the peer group, it was easier for the young person to talk through any problems or personal concerns on matters not necessarily 'spiritual', which we could discuss and then apply biblical principles.

3) On a group level this has enabled the leaders to be able to plan the term's programme with a far greater awareness of the spiritual state of the group as a whole, and adjust our level of teaching appropriately.

It has not always been easy to find time to develop this scheme, but the benefits and effects have been great — the most thrilling being when one lad used the opportunity to give his life to Christ.

Reflecting on our experience, it does seem that the 'Baxter Model' is invaluable as a scheme for pastoring young people, as well as often being a great encouragement for the pastor.

Daniel Rutherford
St Peter's, Harold Wood

NOTE

[1] Richard Baxter, *The Reformed Pastor* (SCM, London 1956), p.109.

ORTHOS
Other Papers already published by Fellowship of Word and Spirit

1
The Rule of Christ and the Kingdom of God
Paul Gardner

2★
The Future Roles of Priests and Laity in Christian Ministry
James Rushton

3★
Ordination for Whom?
An examination of some of the biblical texts relevant to women's ordination
Paul Gardner

4•
Power Evangelism
A pastoral and theological assessment of John Wimber's teaching
Wallace Benn & Mark Burkill

5•
Signs and Wonders in the New Testament
Rowland Moss

6
New Testament Commentaries
A bibliography for evangelical pastors and students
Paul Gardner

7★
Ordination for What?
A consideration of the reality at the heart of the church
Alec Motyer

8•
Healing in the New Testament: Some General Conclusions
Rowland Moss

9
Aspects of Authority
In our message · In our preaching and counselling · In our decision-making
James Packer

10
The Problem of Eternal Punishment
James Packer

11
Recovering the Word
The need for expository preaching today
James Philip

12
The Church in the Age of the TV Image
Dare we still preach?
Simon Vibert

★ Reprinted together under the title *The Church's Ministry*
• Reprinted together under the title *Evangelicals and the Miraculous*

Fellowship of Word and Spirit is a registered charity, no. 293159